MW01258198

This book belongs to:

____

Made in the USA
Las Vegas, NV
17 December 2022

63139562R00066